I HAS A HOTDOG!

I HAS

WHAT YOUR DOG IS REALLY THINKING

Professor Happycat & ihasahotdog.com

GRAND CENTRAL
PUBLISHING

NEW YORK   BOSTON

Grand Central Publishing
Hachette Book Group
237 Park Avenue
New York, NY 10017

www.HachetteBookGroup.com

Printed in China

First Edition: April 2010
10 9 8 7 6 5 4 3 2 1

Grand Central Publishing is a division of Hachette Book Group, Inc.
The Grand Central Publishing name and logo is a trademark of Hachette Book Group, Inc.

Library of Congress Control Number: 2009939096
ISBN: 978-0-446-56638-4

Cover design by Ben Gibson

Dedicated to all of the dogs, puppies, and goggies of the world.

Acknowledgments

Professor Happycat and his staff would like to thank each and every canine contributor to this groundbreaking manual. Though he may not be happy to admit it, this book would not be possible without them. He would also like to thank their humans for their hospitality and lemonade.

I'z watchin u,
stuffed puppeh.
Dun try nuffin

FLAVR?
Mai noz hav itz!

i can has a kiss now?

Beagle
and
Coffee

I pick u

escuse me
i haz kweshun

Thunnerstormz
change evverthing

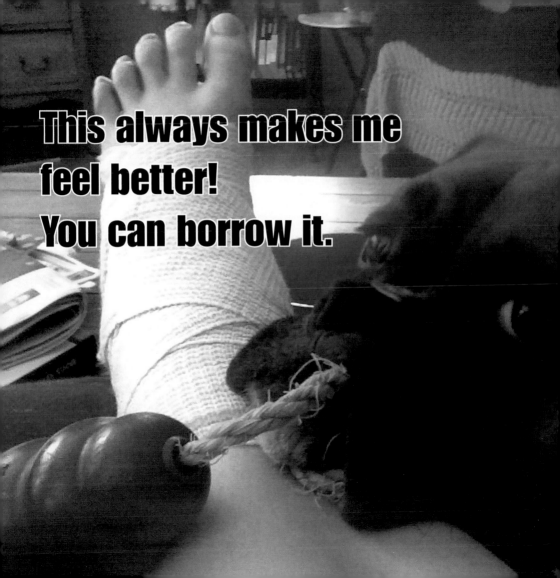

Loldogs now in convenient pocket size

This is
how I roll

invisible p'sgetti kiss

Wh . . . What kinna snacks?

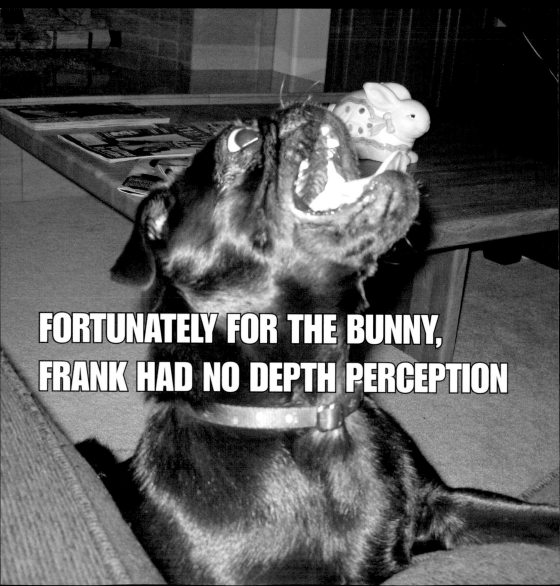

I can has mimosa wif hotdog?

The
last thing
a hotdog
ever sees

kay—we fetched BIG stick fur u . . .
turn on hotdog machine now?

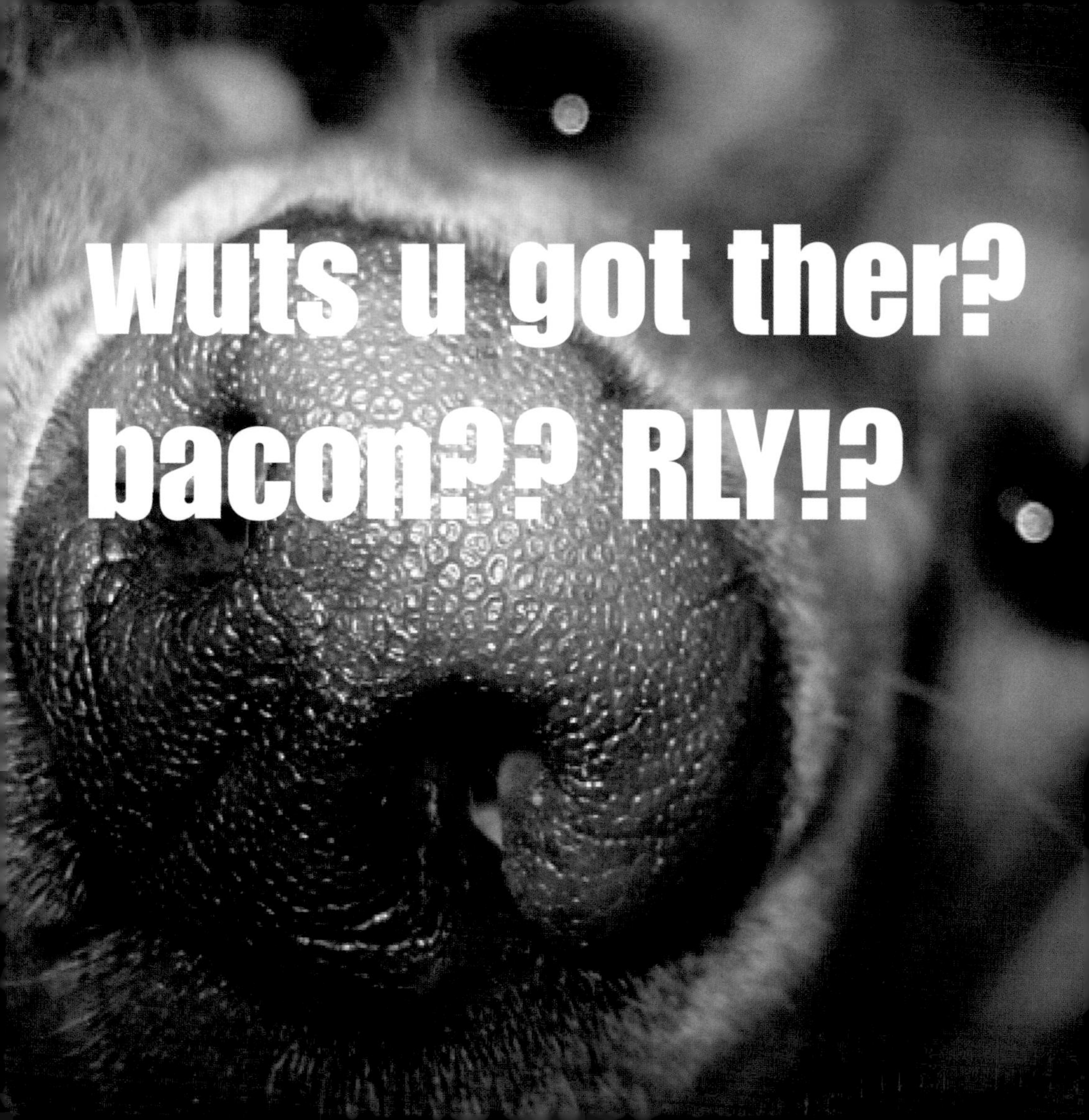
wuts u got ther?
bacon?? RLY!?

Countdown to Nom

3 . . . 2 . . . 1 . . .

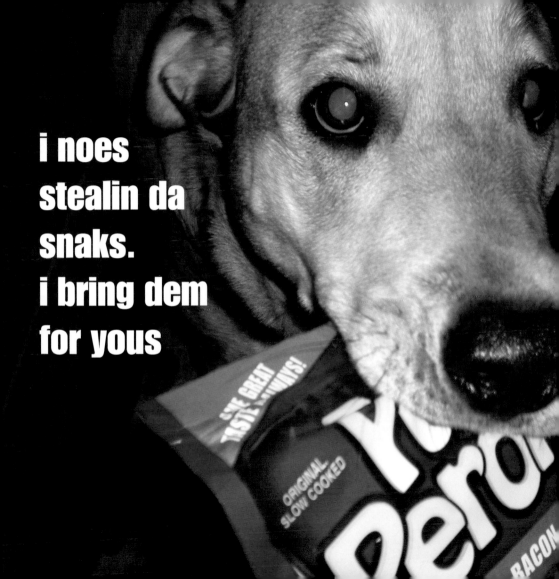

Your offerings are adequate

Do Not Want

Yay . . . . .

your gormay fud
does not pleze me

For this I kill you in your sleep

If I wish real hard
maybe this trip won't end at the vet's

Oh . . .

it's YOU again . . .

1. **Take picture**
2. **Send to Grandma**
3. **Shred sweater, K?**

Dang! Grampz wuznt lyin! Itz uphil, in teh sno, bof waiz

Obedience
School?
Ummmm . . . . . .

NO.

. . . You're kidding rite?

hotdog withdrawl . . . not pretty

This touching scene is one static shock away from being an all-out brawl.

Curiosity may
have killed
the cat,
but for a while
this was our
prime suspect.

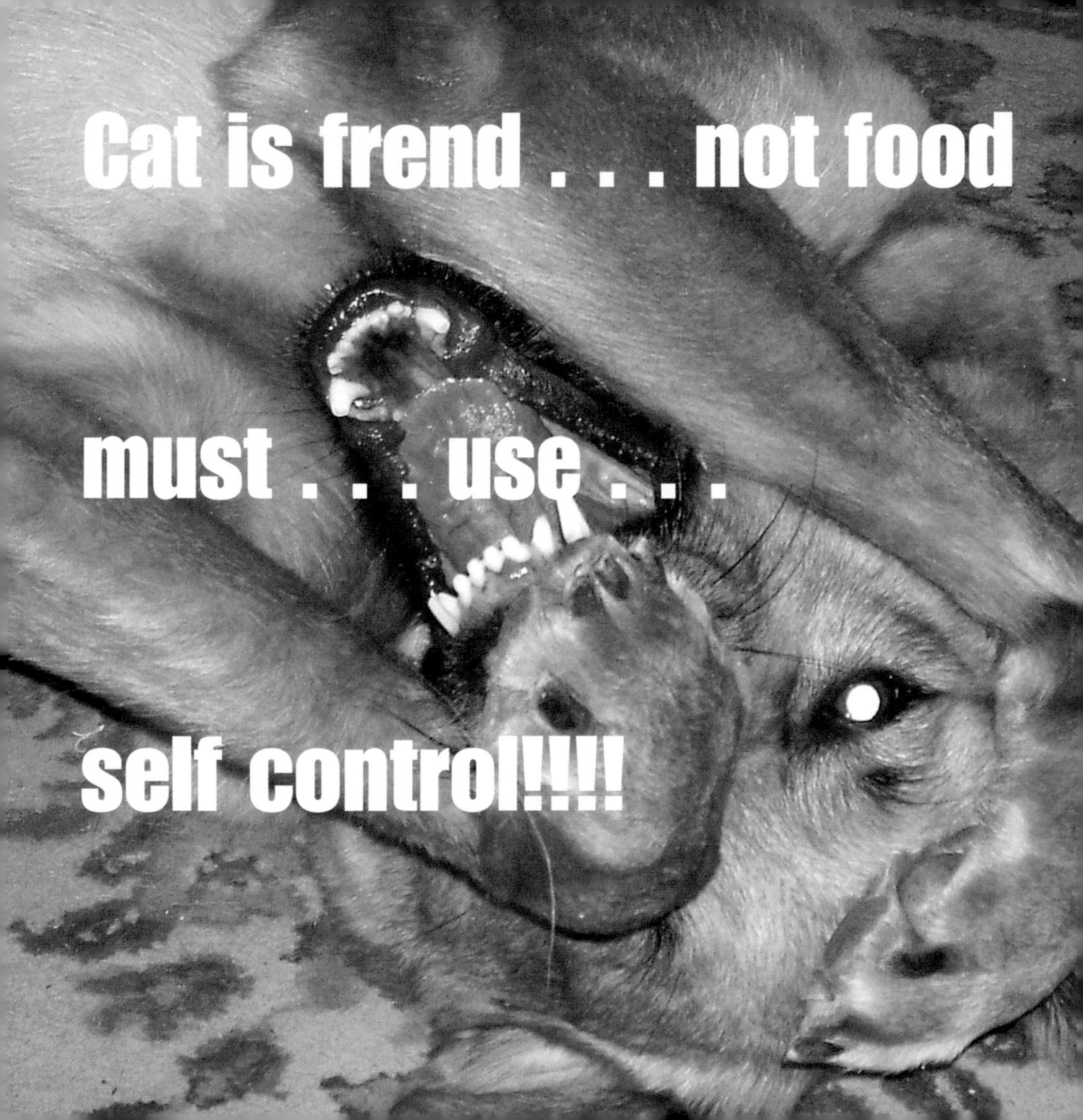
Cat is frend . . . not food
must . . . use . . .
self control!!!!

evil pug

anticupatn

cat's flavor

If de cat getz dat big . . .

Iz gonna need backups

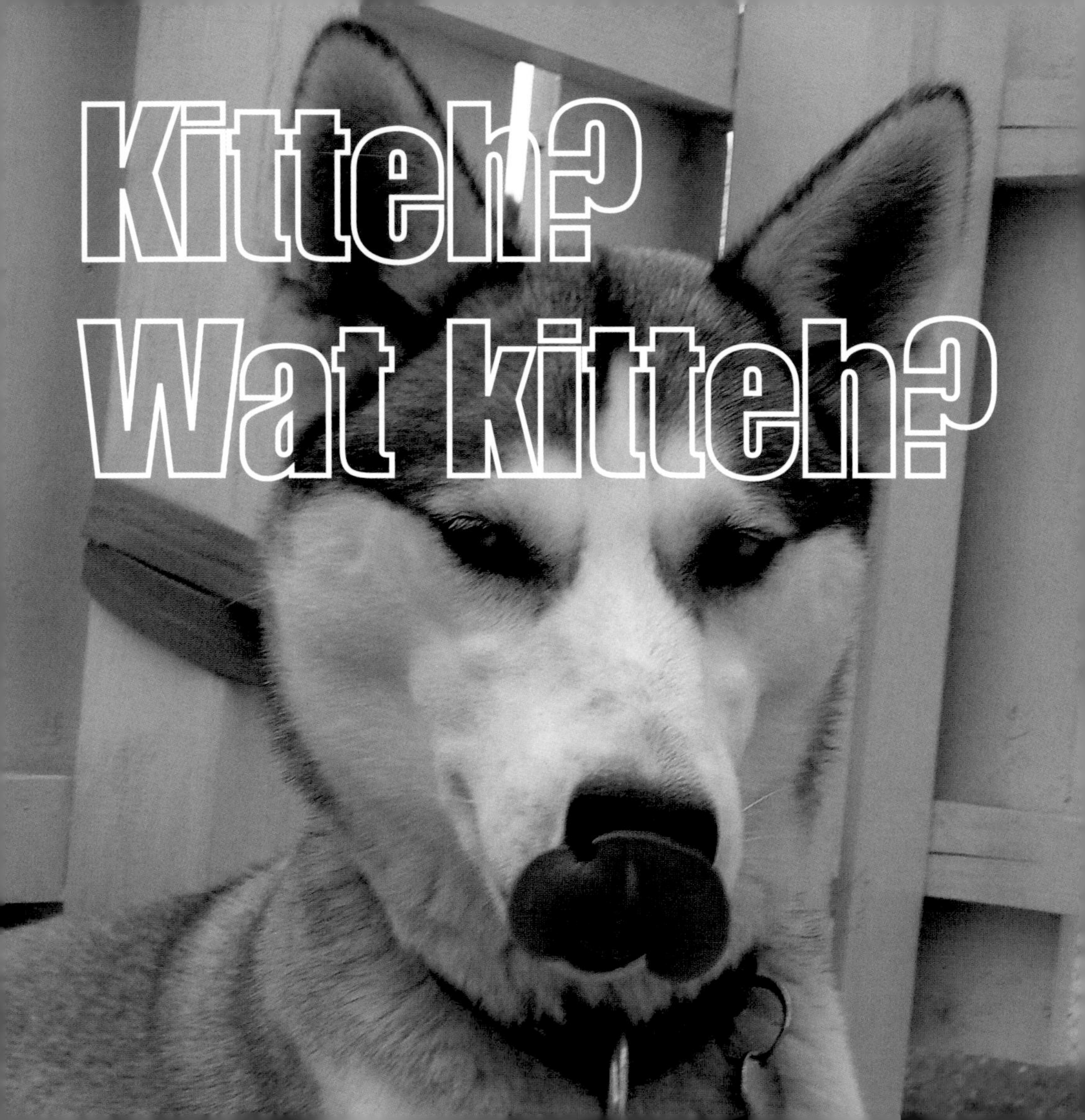
Kitteh?
Wat kitteh?

I know June is
Adopt a Shelter Cat Month.
I'll take two
with mustard.

Brain

Iz adopted?

OMG . . .

FROSTING!!!!!!!!

not like in car
but close

Mom sed I iz gifted

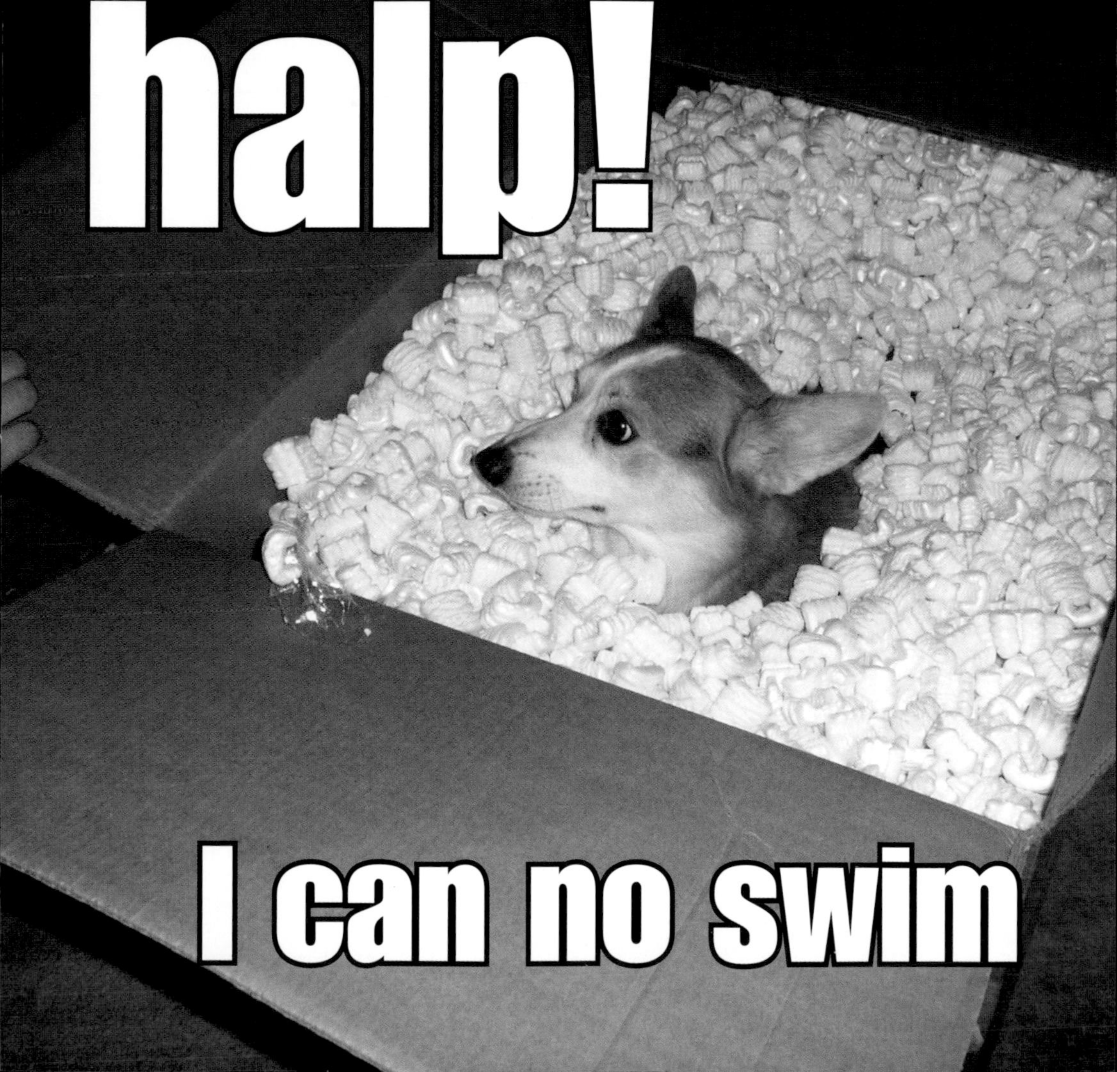
halp!
I can no swim

Goggie not 2 big for lap
Lap 2 small for goggie

5 o'clock shadow

I got yur back dude

Who sez blondes have moar fun?

They said walk da hooman
Neva anything bout
bringing em bak

Teknikally...
I still on ground

Trouble

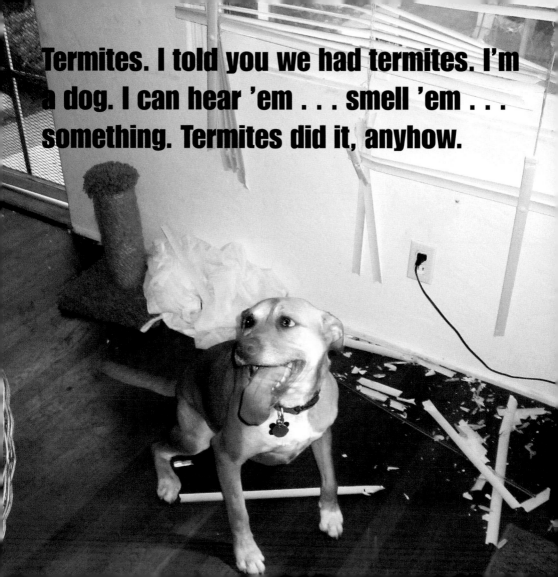

Momdog
duz nawt beleev
ur storee

INNOCENT DOGGIE

is as shocked as you are that your shoes fell apart when u put them on

why, yes . . .

i DID maek dis mess, fanks fer noticin

. . . but you stil wuv me rite?

Oh hai!
Did you know . . .
dis magazine
has a flavr

At least I behave better than your 401(k)

I'm in yer Pool
Sharin my Drool.

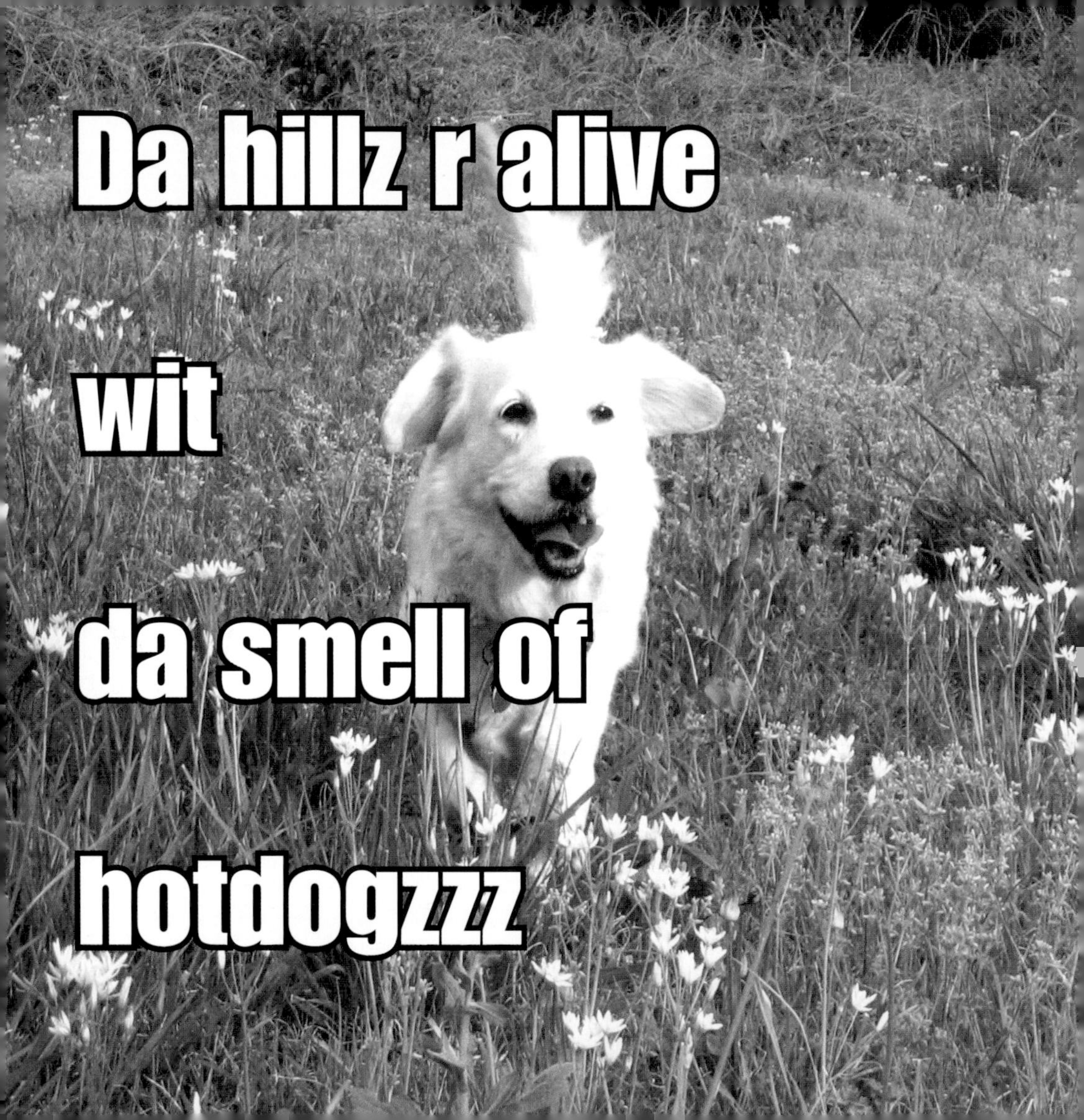
Da hillz r alive
wit
da smell of
hotdogzzz

But teh toy
cannot trow itself

Ready for doubles?

iz saving u
from a large,
fluffy lobster

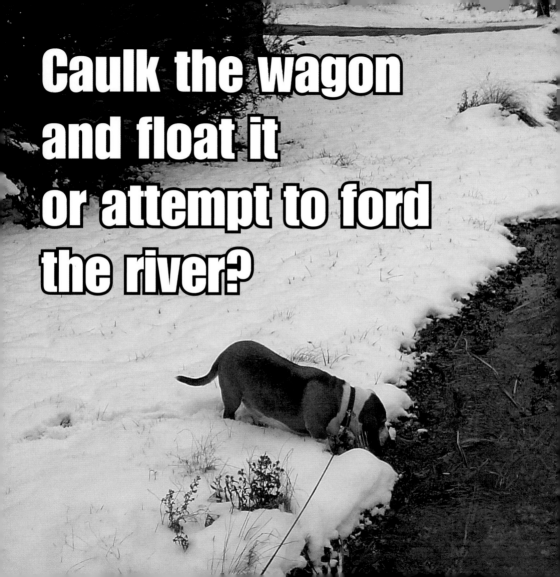

True friends stick together

i gettin up . . .
soon . . . ish . . .

your chances of a long nap are spotty at best

i had a sleepee 'n it wun

I'm in ur bedz
sheddinz on
ur blankiez . . .
'nd droolin
on ur pillowz

SECURITY SYSTEM DISARMED

HIS HERS

Can I sleep wif yoos?

I even sleepz cute

Chased 2 cars, dug 3 holes, barked at the mailman and the meter reader, protected house from the evil joggers, took you for a long walk

It's been a long day

PRODUCTION CREDITS: WRITING & EDITING: SONYA VATOMSKY & BEN HUH
CHAPTER ILLUSTRATIONS: JOE RUFA

Cute

Caption	Credit
but don i looks pretty?	Kevin, Ashley & Montemarie "Baloney" Dougherty
Ladeez . . . Enuff 4 everyonz	Nadya Dooley
I'z watchin u, stuffed puppeh.	Brian, Misti and Misha
Dun try nuffin	
FLAVR? Mai noz hav itz!	
I drawded u a love . . .	Lickspittle Fang—Zombie Dog Extraordinaire!
Yes, Al helps wit Easter eggz. Wy u ask?	Jacqueline and Biscuit
I can has a kiss now?	Ginger's Huminz and Gizmo
	Kaycee "Li'l Little" Sawran—Professional Deer Chaser—shouting out to her peeps, Chris, Wendee, Nala, Baylee, Bear & Benny
I would like to speek to the Hugs Department, plz?	Kalae Casorso—proud mommy to Champ!
Beagle and Coffee	Paul & Samantha Johnson and Murray Lynn & Molly Mae—our beagles
cuddles time yet?	Scott Beattie and Corto
I leks kibbles, and hotdogs, and long walks on beach . . .	Lucy on the beach, by Allison Parsley
I pick u	Vanessa Putt
Tells it again . . . 'Bout Princess and Pea	Emilie and Dharma
Insert Hotdog Here———>	Dukes Doggie's proud owner is Robyn Andrews; he's the best impulse buy she has ever made! Dukes loves running with his Mommy and loves to ham it up and make his way into lots of photos . . . and he's still waiting for his hotdog!!!
kthxbye	
escuse me	MiaBellalagotto.co.nz
i haz kwestiun	
i u	Ebba Nilson & Rufus
I stick my tongue at u sir	Heather Rhodes and Genny
Thunnerstormz change everthing	Monika Weitkunat
This always makes me feel better! You can borrow it.	Emily Silver, lover of toasted marshmallows, & Knuckles the oggie
my furst photo shoot how dispose?	Sandi Pearce and Mr. Mojo Risin'!
I put all ma toyz away . . . can I have ice cream now?	Annika Toth and Sadie
Sry can't heer you over sound of hao awesome i am.	Polo Noble, an Imperial Toy Shih-tzu owned by Paulette Cooper Noble & Paul Noble. Photo by Tina Valente.
dont mind me, I'll just sit here in the cold	Dozer (Maltese/Yorkie)—Owners: Chris and Jessica Weber
Loldogs	Heather——www. everythingunderthemoon.net
now in convenient pocket size	Ron——www.fastcoolcras.net
He's still watching me isn't he?	Speck Esbia Esq. by Patti Esbia
This is how I roll	Beverly Dawn Hembree
Why I eated so many hotdogs?	To the Cooper family for making our dogs so special, especially pugs!
	The puppies in the photo are brother "Arthur" and his sister "Amelie v.'t Hazelwoud." Breeder: Jester Nathalie Spek Kennel:
i kiss it mak it better?	"v.'t Hazelwoud," website http://nathaliesteckels.come2me.nl/ Country: Netherlands
	Butters <3 Tango and their wonderful parents Jillian Schoenfeld, Marc Green, Anita Seguiti, and Matt Burkhalter
invisible p'sgetti kiss	

Food

Caption	Credit
Happy birfday to me?	Photo by Carrie Mooney—"Sissy Ohlivia Mooney"
Cakes	Jeanne Turschmann
They make everyone happy.	
Almost.	
LE NOM!!!	Buckley & Daman Hoffman
Wh . . . What kinna snacks?	Stella
FORTUNATELY FOR THE BUNNY, FRANK HAD NO DEPTH PERCEPTION	Rosy Glazer—Black Pug. Photo by Scott Glazer. Owners: Peter & Cyndie Glazer. Nicknames: Rocket, Monster, Bargain.
I can has mimosa wif hotdog?	Kim Hoffman and Bentley Vicino
no rly, i keep box safe	Pebbles by Scuba (Stephen Sigward)
Fud? Fud? Fud?	Abhy's mom, Katie
All dis for me? Oh, I couldn't. Well, actually, I coulds. Should I waits for da buns or should I starts now?	Kristi, Kevin, and Brenden the Super-Dog
The last thing a hotdog ever sees	Cassandra The Great—Aunt Dea to Famous Amos. I love you, Aaron, Jacques & Rocky!
It's the rest of the fry or most of your fingers. Up to you.	Victoria Escamilla and her dog, Shadow
While yur up . . . how bout sum noms?	Photo by Kathleen and Gimli Pigwidgeon Murphy's mom Carol McEachern-Murphy

Caption	Credit
iz soo cold but . . . iz soo good	Donna Balsdon and Lily the Singing Dog (http://youtube.com/watch?v=3TecsTheIrs)
kay—we fetched Big stick fur u . . . turn on hotdog machine now?	Photo by: Ben Perego. Dog owned by: Meghan Moran & Ben Perego.
wuts u got ther? bacon?? RLY?	Aaron Przybylski & Dolly being babysat
Currently i iz just looking	Fauna's proud parents: Dani and Tyrell
Countdown to Nom 3 . . . 2 . . . 1 . . .	Edfromjersey (Sammy)
dis? oh dis iz mai new fud dish, wat? u didn't git de memo?	silver22 and Loki
Self-Control i has it.	Vera, Mommy, and Aunt Lindsey
i noes stealin da snaks. i bring dem for yous	Alex Stanglewicz and Sophie
Your offerings are adequate	Gus The Dog
No More Txts fud bowlz empty	Tiffany Pickering's Baby Koopa

Caption	Credit

Do Not Want

Caption	Credit
Yay	Rory and Kelli McAllister & Penelope
your gurmay fud does not pleze me	Johannes and Ada Mae. Photo by Sarah Brotwahl.
revenge I will haz it	Lori, Billy & Monte
For this I kill you in your sleep	Ankie's and Moo's puppy, Charlie
If I wish real hard maybe this trip won't end at the vet's	Jeniter Caisman
Oh . . . it's YOU again . . .	Geena Matala
1. Take picture 2. Send to Grandma 3. Shred sweater, K?	Dustin & Jackie. Banesi Dog Name; Pennie (aka: Snoop).
Un. . . . wayter? Iz orderd mah steak rare . . . not kibbled.	Ally and Terra
FUN! fun? not fun	Brandon Tuott and Ein
Bang! Gramz wuznt tyin! Itz uphil, in teh sno, bof waiz	Cory Brunner
da crismuz bfooz . . . . . . i has it.	Andrea Skantar and Oz
Obedience School? Unmmm . . . . . . NO.	Ian Southward
Shhh . . . iz bath time. I iz pretending to be statue.	Big Z loves Kali & Dude
. . . You're kidding rite?	Beverly Dawn Hembree
Is she chewing WHITE shoes after Labor Day???	George Rudd and Mina
Kat put Krazy Glue on plant. Again.	Miss Sadie S. Pie Bell by Florence Yue. Rebirthed by Richard C. Bell

Kill Cat

Caption	Credit
This touching scene is one static shock away from being an all-out brawl.	Stephen & Sarah Amerino & the boys!
Curiosity may have killed the cat, but for a while this was our prime suspect.	Bret Robinson
Oh corse U noe, dis meenz war. nom nom nommi.	Jacqueline and Keith Brooks
got rid of cat and nobody knows it but me	Nancy Bird and Footz
quik. load teh kitteh! teh hooman iz commin!	Jay Chrisman
Cat is frend . . . not food must . . . use . . . self control!!!	Gretchen Phillips
evil pug anticypatn cat's flavor did somebody say something? get of uv meh u lump!	Annie Hoyt For my parents, Gary and Kathy Young. Love, Robyn
It de gez dat big . . . Iz gonna need backups	http://www.griefandrecovery.com Katie Atherton and Ruby-roo
Kitteh? Wat kitteh?	Russel
quicksand! halp! . . . no	The Bipolar Cookie
Been workin' this beat 3 years now We got real problem wif bad kittehs	Judi, Tessie, and Larry Ludwar Marsha V Morlock and Mistah Chu, King of the Universe and Champion Snorer
TEH TRUTH sumtimez herts	Hope and her beloved Reba, the best CBR ever
wut kitteh? i dun seee a kitteh.	JNX and SCREAMER "YIN YANG WE HAZ IT"

Caption	Credit
hotdog withdrawl. . . . . not pretty	Michael Forest Veredas MFVPhotography.com
plz help meh!	Photo by Michelle Rush, Princess, age 4. Chesapeake Bay Retriever/Chow (?) Mix. Very patient with children . . . (obviously)
My accommodations are very inadequate	Barbara Reike and Stella
Urge ta kil . . . Rising . . .	Amanda Arnold, Daniel Graber, and Loki
No one haz friended me on Facebook ha ha ha!!!1 it sound like you jus sed wez getting a kat. why you not tarting?	Croissant and Kristin Beers Laura Slack In memory of Maggie Moo Moo (1993–2008)

Caption	Credit
I know June is Adopt a Shelter Cat Month. I'll take two with mustard.	Michael Hawk

Caption	Credit
Iz adopted?	Kim Williamson, Monica Williams & Shelley Saindon, in memory of Kokomo and Bert
OMG . . . FROSTING!!!!!!	Megan and Chris Schommer (& Winnie the Corgi)
not like in car but close	Susan Flayer (and Jake)
Mom sed I iz gifted	Tyler Brown
halp! I can no swim	Guiness (the dog), Brooke & Andrew
sandwich pretty gud ackshully	Evellen Potze
Just fine-tuning my antennae.	Celeste Risko and Bella Mia, an Italian Greyhound
But u has a ham sammich and I has NO ham sammich	Beverly Dawn Hembree
I didn't hit you . . . I high-fived your face!!	Phyllis Rhodes
teh rainbo i tastes it!	Jennifer McKelfley and Bandit
Momma . . . Dis no look lyk da park . . .	Andrea Cleland
Me is INCOGCHEETO	Sara Dykes and Orson the Dogge at www.youtube.com/user/orsondogge
Fixed? I no broken.	Aerish, Casper & Grace
I stayz heer. Rok eezier 2 herd.	Michael Kaufman
This disguise is great! She'll never recognize me!	Gregorio Litenstein and Mack
Mailman, wait! I overslept! I have to chase you!	The Sommers Family: Sam, Debbie, Benjamin, Allison & Josh, with Lady, Daisy Lou & Lilly
Goggie no! 2 big for lap / Lap 2 small for goggie / I feel dis a trap / but I no mind	Brittany Vaughn and Lancelot
5 o'clock shadow	Jake & Amanda Catangelo
A tree! I FOUND A TREE! now I can pee	Anna Korzhavina and Richard Kehoe
I got yer back dude	Thanks to Cujo and Deja Vu, Mark, Jack, and the rest of the South Euclid Dog Park crew. Liz :)
Who sez blondes have moar fun?	Janice Wilkins, Donna Brooks, Dahlia

Caption	Credit
Iz been licking licking licking! tung wore owt. trying reel hard, but teh boan haz no flava at awt.	Dave, Kim, Loki & Mel Slagle
Down! Down! Curse you, magic window!	Bret Robinson
Weiner envy	Tyler Brown
I has it.	
U said: "Stay off da KITCHEN table!" I shall call him . . . Mini me	Brandi & Bazil Not Bayzil / Masie Jorgensen
Dude, you EAT this stuff? Don't you want a hotdog or somethin'?	Debbie Bucciero and puppeh Simon!
vet said he was sick me no haf to go?	Grace Kavinsky and her true-hearted goggie, Scout
They said walk da hooman Neva anything bout bringing em bak	Ruben Giró and Daina
Teknikally . . . I still on ground	Corey Hicks

Caption	Credit
oh ya . . . it waz worf it	Kathy, Glenn, and Duke
Termites. I told you we had termites. I'm a dog. I can hear 'em . . . smell 'em . . . something. Termites did it, anyhow.	Annie O'Brien and Mudslide, featuring Jane's mini-blinds
Temptation . . . thy name is shoe	Deri Pryor and Ozzy
No worries! Dis one from mean naybor's garden.	Ashley Street and Ringo
Cat did it! I swur!	
Momdog duz nawt beleev ur storee	Mollie—by Adam Green photography
I'z in your flowerbeds . . . Nom'ing your perenials	Jon Kroener and Michelle Yotter
It waz getting ready to attack and . . .	Bo and the Brinkman Family
. . . What donut?	Sam and Allie Garza and Miss Lily
you're welcome	
Oh hai! I gotz da mail!	Sarah Magness, Carrie Whitworth, and Sophie the Pug / I, Adele Penelope Moore, send a special shout-out to big brother Oscar and mom and dad, Lauren & Matt Shaver, for their continuous love and support—even during my more trying times.
So many flowers to dig up . . . So little time . . . we wuz trying to stop the cat	Roxy & her family: Bob, Lisa, Jennica, & Kyle Smith / Beth, Rob, Matilda, Quigley & Coconut Morency
Ralph, it's a cop! Act natural.	Chris and his Jesshire Cat
INNOCENT DOGGIE is as shocked as you are that your shoes fell apart when u put them on	Erma and Joie Stangland—Flower!! Look—COWS!
u kilid a man? we just pee on floorz.	Evellen Potze